This Journal Belongs To:

_____

Date

THE ART OF RON DICIANNI

Any picture can make you look—ours will help you see.

A prophet's tears, a father's prayers, angels keeping watch...
An artist whose heart is evident through the work of his hands,
Ron DiCianni's paintings have been enormously successful in reaching
and awakening the spirituality of thousands of art collectors worldwide.

Ron's work has won him national recognition with many national
corporations, including the commission as official artist for the
United States Olympic Committee for the Moscow Olympic Games.
He has since dedicated his talents solely to the task of proclaiming
the "Good News" of the Gospel.

Ron's credits include cover illustrations for This Present Darkness,
Piercing the Darkness, Angelwalk and is the creator and illustrator of the
award-winning "Tell Me..." series. Ron has recently authored Beyond
Words, a collection of his favorite paintings with personal devotions.

For more information on the images in this journal or any of
Ron DiCianni's work, please call 1-800-391-1136 or visit us online at
www.art2see.com.

ISBN: 1-57051-397-X

Text © 1999 The Brownlow Corporation.
6309 Airport Freeway
Fort Worth, Texas 76117

FOR THIS CHILD I PRAY

A FATHER PRAYS

FOR HIS CHILDREN

Featuring the Artwork of
RON DiCIANNI

*

Written by
JOHN & BRENDA WARD

Brownlow

CONTENTS

The Power of a Father's Prayer

God has blessed fathers with the high calling of providing spiritual maturity and stability for their homes. As part of this preeminent responsibility, we are (1) to model God's unconditional love to our dear children He has given, and (2) to teach and encourage them to love God and seek His will. Nothing else will ever be as important.

But how are we to accomplish all this? We can't do it by ourselves, and the sooner we realize this the better. God's power and God's protection stand ready to enable us as we seek His will and turn our hearts to prayer.

To prayer! That is the only way fathers will ever be able to fulfill their God-given responsibility.

This practical journal, inspired by Hannah's tender prayer for her son (1 Samuel 1:27) and Ron DiCianni's powerful art, will help provide a focus as you pray for your children regularly. As you go through the 52 helpful themes, you will notice several features:

⁕We need to praise God before we present our requests. God wants a relationship wiht us; He doesn't want to merely listen to people beg for stuff.

⁕We need to pray for ourselves before we pray for our children. How else can we model and teach forgiveness, patience and holiness until we have grown in it (not mastered it) ourselves? I must pray for myself, *God's child,* before I pray for *my child.* It's harder this way, but trust God. This is the way He planned it.

✳We need to remember it is never too early to pray for our child's future development, character, or spouse. No matter your child's age—20 months or 20 years—the general themes in this journal will still be relevant. Depending on your child's present age, you will merely be changing the specifics of your prayer.

You can make this journal a private matter between yourself and God, or you can write in such a way as to leave it for your children some day as a treasured gift. Both ways are helpful and good. Use one format one year, the other the next.

Often, as fathers, we spend more time in worry for our children than in prayer. Worry is real; we can feel it and somehow believe we are at least *doing* something. But wouldn't it be better to worry less and pray more? And when we do, God is honored, our lives are blessed and our children are shielded by the power and protection of God Almighty.

A FATHER'S NEED FOR PRAYER

Devote yourselves to prayer.
1 CORINTHIANS 7:5

"I'll pray for you." All too often we say these words like we were saying, "Have a nice day."
We not only minimize the importance of prayer but also its power in our lives.
Our children will only learn that prayer matters if it matters to us. We must model
a healthy relationship with our Heavenly Father if we want our children to have one.
That means making prayer a priority and not an afterthought.

Set aside time each day and pray. Then watch the impact on your family.

HEAVENLY FATHER, AS *YOUR* CHILD I PRAY...

Dear Father, thank You for...

I ask for Your present and future guidance in praying for these specific needs in my family...

HEAVENLY FATHER, FOR MY CHILD I PRAY...

As a father, I ask that You place a burden on my heart to pray for these areas of my child's life...

_____

_____

_____

_____

_____

_____

_____

Today God, may my child begin to understand the importance of prayer as he/she...

_____

_____

_____

_____

_____

_____

_____

_____

And in the future, Lord...

_____

_____

_____

_____

_____

_____

_____

Pray for my soul. More things are wrought by prayer than this world dreams of.
ALFRED, LORD TENNYSON

DEALING WITH ANGER

In your anger, do not sin.
Do not let the sun go down while you are still angry.
EPHESIANS 4:26

Anger is an extremely powerful emotion. When used appropriately it can yield
equally powerful results. But it can also cause a lot of damage and if turned inward can lead
to bitterness. Let your anger fire you, not control you. And don't go to bed mad.

See Psalm 4:4.

HEAVENLY FATHER, AS YOUR CHILD I PRAY...

Dear Father, thank You for helping me stay in control of my anger even when...

I ask for Your present and future guidance in understanding my anger and...

HEAVENLY FATHER, FOR MY CHILD I PRAY...

As a father, I pray for strength not to lose my temper when...

Today God, help my child be in control of his/her temper even when...

And in the future, Lord...

I never work better than when I am inspired by anger; for when I am angry,
I can write, pray and preach well, for then my whole temperament is quickened,
my understanding sharpened, and all mundane vexations and temptations depart.
MARTIN LUTHER

THE GRATEFUL LIVING

*Let the word of Christ dwell in you richly as you teach
and admonish one another with all wisdom,
and as you sing psalms, hymns and spiritual songs
with gratitude in your hearts to God.*

COLOSSIANS 3:16

*What am I truly thankful for? Is it health? Is it my family? These are wonderful things and
surely we should be grateful for all of them, but gratitude is a state of the heart. It calls us to be
mindful of the smallest thing and where it came from. And it starts with two little words:
"thank you." And if my children are to learn gratitude, they must see it in me.*

HEAVENLY FATHER, AS *YOUR* CHILD I PRAY...

Dear Father, thank You for blessings in my life such as...

I ask for Your present and future guidance in learning to be more grateful to my family as they...

Heavenly Father, For My Child I Pray...

As a father, I pray for the ability to model gratitude in even the smallest ways of...

Today God, help my child learn to show gratitude to others as...

And in the future, Lord...

When it comes to life, the critical thing is whether you take things
for granted or take them with gratitude.
G. K. CHESTERTON

A Father's Time

I hope to spend some time with you.

1 CORINTHIANS 16:7

Of all of the resources that we have to spend, time is one that can never be replenished.
It is absolutely critical that we spend that time on the things that matter the most.
As a father we all know very well that it is not just the quality of time but also the quantity
of time that we spend with our children that will ultimately make a huge impact on their lives.
We show them what is important to us by where we spend our time.

HEAVENLY FATHER, AS YOUR CHILD I PRAY...

Dear Father, thank You for always taking the time to listen to me when I...

_____

_____

_____

_____

_____

_____

_____

_____

I ask for Your present and future guidance in protecting my time from...

_____

_____

_____

_____

_____

_____

Heavenly Father, For My Child I Pray...

As a father, I pray for discernment in knowing where and how to use my time in...

Today God, help my child learn to enjoy the present moment as he/she is...

And in the future, Lord...

Love is extravagant in the price it is willing to pay, the time it is willing to give...
and the strength it is willing to spend.

JONI EARECKSON TADA

STRESS FRACTURES

Seek peace and pursue it.
PSALM 34:14

The Lord blesses his people with peace.
PSALM 29:11

We've all felt it; we know what it is, and probably live with a healthy dose of it daily.
Stress is a constant in our world, and unfortunately we have learned to live with it.
But how do we respond to stress if it has become commonplace? We can't always stop it.
We can't ignore it. But we can give it to God and ask Him for the peace to make it through.

HEAVENLY FATHER, AS YOUR CHILD I PRAY...

Dear Father, thank You for helping me through these stressful times of...

_____

_____

_____

_____

_____

_____

_____

I ask for Your present and future guidance in reducing stress as my family faces...

_____

_____

_____

_____

HEAVENLY FATHER, FOR My CHILD I PRAY...

As a father, I pray for discernment in recognizing the early warning signs of stress such as...

_____

_____

_____

_____

_____

_____

_____

Today God, help my child respond in a Godly, peaceful way when...

_____

_____

_____

_____

_____

And in the future, Lord...

_____

_____

_____

_____

_____

_____

_____

My only advice is to stay aware, listen carefully, and yell for help if you need it.
JUDY BLUME

GENTLE MEN

Let your gentleness be evident to all.

PHILIPPIANS 4:5

Few things are more tender than a baby. Unless, of course, we count the hearts
of the parents who have just looked on that baby for the first time. Or, perhaps,
they have just watched their baby get on a school bus for the first time.
Life is filled with gentleness, and some of us are better at it than others. But God will give
each of us more gentleness and tenderness as we pray for and practice them.

HEAVENLY FATHER, AS YOUR CHILD I PRAY...

Dear Father, thank You for the gentleness You show me even when...

_____
_____
_____
_____
_____
_____

I ask for more gentleness in dealing with my family on the issue of...

_____
_____
_____
_____
_____
_____

HEAVENLY FATHER, FOR MY CHILD I PRAY...

As a father, I pray for the ability to model gentleness as I...

_____

_____

_____

_____

_____

_____

Today God, help my child develop a tender heart as...

_____

_____

_____

_____

_____

_____

_____

_____

And in the future, Lord...

_____

_____

_____

_____

_____

_____

_____

A child's hand in yours—what tenderness and power it arouses.
You are instantly the very touchstone of wisdom and strength.
MARJORIE HOLMES

Parent and Teacher—All in One

In your teaching show integrity
and seriousness.

TITUS 2:7

From the day they come into the world we begin to teach them. And our children
are sponges, ready to soak up everything that we, and others, expose them to.
So, we must be careful. They learn as much from what they see us do as they learn
from what we say. We must remember, class never dismisses.

Heavenly Father, As Your Child I Pray...

Dear Father, thank You for teaching me...

I ask for Your present and future guidance as I teach my family...

HEAVENLY FATHER, FOR MY CHILD I PRAY...

As a father, I pray for wisdom in how to teach these specific things...

Today God, help my child see the value of learning as he/she...

And in the future, Lord...

There is so much to teach, and the time goes so fast.
ERMA BOMBECK

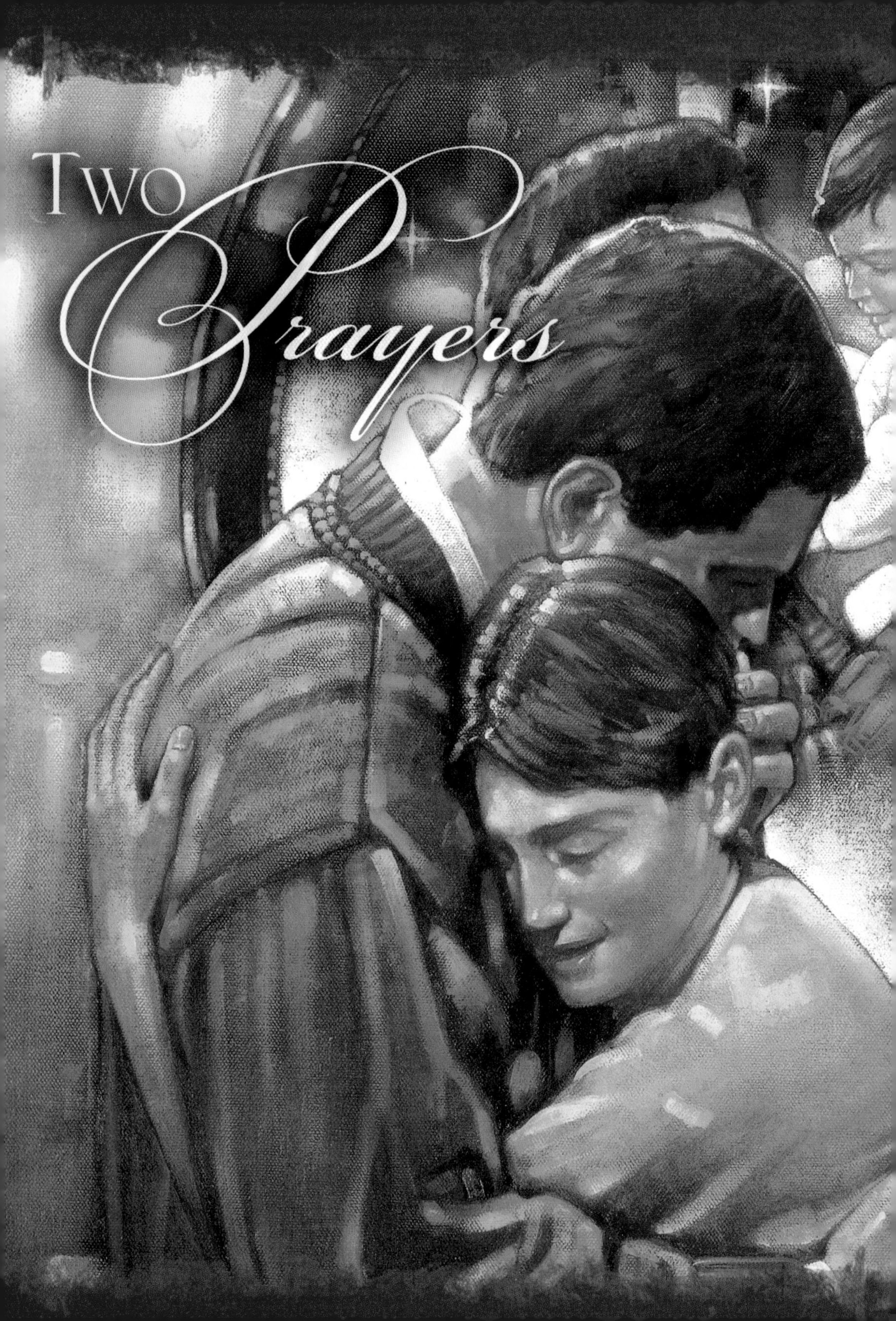

Two
Prayers

Last night my little boy confessed to me

Some childish wrong;

And kneeling at my knee,

He prayed with tears—

"Dear God, make me a man

Like Daddy—wise and strong;

I know you can."

Then while he slept

I knelt beside his bed,

Confessed my sins,

And prayed with low-bowed head

"O God make me a child

Like my child here—

Pure, guileless,

Trusting Thee with faith sincere."

ANDREW GILLIES

A FATHER'S HANDS

Fathers, do not exasperate your children; instead,
bring them up in the training and instruction of the Lord.
EPHESIANS 6:4

I have never felt more responsibility than when I was standing in the delivery room holding a newborn daughter! A father has no greater responsibility than to hold another's life in his own—physically, emotionally and spiritually.

Accepting this kind of responsibility is just part of being a Dad. We can't dismiss the role we have been placed in without severe consequences both to ourselves and to our children.

HEAVENLY FATHER, AS YOUR CHILD I PRAY...

Dear Father, forgive me for being irresponsible in...

I ask for Your present and future guidance in becoming more responsible in these areas...

Heavenly Father, For My Child I Pray...

As a father, I pray for ways to teach my children responsibility in these specific areas...

Today God, help my child desire to be responsible in even small ways such as...

And in the future, Lord...

Responsibility is a unique concept. It can only reside and inhere in a
single individual. You may share it with others, but your portion is not diminished.
You may delegate it, but it is still with you.
ADMIRAL RICKOVER

HOLY, HOLY, HOLY

*By one sacrifice God has made perfect forever
those who are being made holy.*

HEBREWS 10:14

Holiness seems like an impossible goal in light of the demands placed on each of us every day.
That is until we realize that becoming holy is an ongoing process that will last the rest
of our lives. God is not interested in our piety or how religious we are.
He just wants us to become more like Him. It's an attitude that guides our thoughts
and decisions throughout the day and not just on Sundays. Sure, we will fail.
But God looks at the heart, and He wants ours to be holy.

✳

HEAVENLY FATHER, AS *YOUR* CHILD I PRAY...

Dear Father, thank You for making me holy through the blood of Jesus even though...

_____

_____

_____

_____

_____

_____

_____

I ask for Your grace to become the holy person You count me as. I need help in...

_____

_____

_____

_____

_____

_____

HEAVENLY FATHER, FOR MY CHILD I PRAY...

As a father, I pray that I will be an example of holy living for my child as...

Today God, help my child want to become holy in the midst of an unholy world. Specifically...

And in the future, Lord...

*Holiness is something below the surface of a life, deep down in the realm
of attitude...and attitude toward God Himself.*
CHUCK SWINDOLL

FAITH OF OUR FATHERS

We always thank God, the Father of our Lord Jesus Christ,
when we pray for you, because we have heard
of your faith and the love you have for all the saints.
COLOSSIANS 1:34

Faith is the childlike confidence and trust that God will do what He has said.
From the very start we have faith. We trust that when we cry, someone will respond
and give us what we need. As we grow, we learn who we can and cannot put our faith in.
But ultimately we must learn that every person will let us down and that God is the only one
in whom we can have complete faith and confidence.

HEAVENLY FATHER, AS YOUR CHILD I PRAY...

Dear Father, thank You for always being there, Eternally Faithful, even when I...

_____

_____

_____

_____

_____

_____

_____

_____

I ask for faith to keep trusting when I...

_____

_____

_____

_____

HEAVENLY FATHER, FOR MY CHILD I PRAY...

As a father, I pray for the ability to model faithfulness to my child as I...

Today God, help my child's faith be strengthened as he/she...

And in the future, Lord...

Faith never knows where it is being led, but it loves and knows the one who is leading.
OSWALD CHAMBERS

HONESTLY NOW!

Do not use dishonest standards. Use honest scales and honest weights. I am the Lord your God who brought you out of Egypt.

LEVITICUS 19:36

Honesty is much more than not telling lies. It is telling the truth—all of it—to God, ourselves, and others. The danger is that when we are totally honest, then we become totally vulnerable. The walls of our creation come down and the real us comes through, bringing a new freedom. If I want my child to be honest, then I must be honest.

HEAVENLY FATHER, AS YOUR CHILD I PRAY...

Dear Father, forgive me for my dishonesty in...

_____

_____

_____

_____

_____

_____

_____

_____

I ask for Your presence and future guidance in making honesty a priority in my home by...

_____

_____

_____

_____

_____

_____

Heavenly Father, For My Child I Pray...

As a father, help me to model honesty for my child in the way I...

Today God, help my child see the value and importance of honesty as he/she...

And in the future, Lord...

Friends, if we be honest with ourselves, we shall be honest with each other.
GEORGE MACDONALD

GROWING PAINS

And Jesus grew in wisdom and stature,
and in favor with God and man.

LUKE 2:52

By God's design, all living things grow. But growth involves more than just the physical body.
We are triune beings, made up of body, mind, and spirit. We must grow in all
these areas to be healthy. Just as our bodies need food, so do our minds and spirits.

Eat healthy, study hard, and pray.
With time and effort and God's help, the result will be growth.

HEAVENLY FATHER, AS YOUR CHILD I PRAY...

Dear Father, thank You for being the Unchanging One, the...

I ask for Your present and future guidance as I strive to grow more like You in...

Heavenly Father, For My Child I Pray...

As a father, I pray for the following areas where I need to grow specifically...

Today God, help my child begin to grow in these areas...

And in the future, Lord...

We can never be lilies in the garden unless we have spent time
as bulbs in the dark, totally ignored.
OSWALD CHAMBERS

INTEGRITY OF HEART

The man of integrity walks securely, but he who takes crooked paths will be found out.

PROVERBS 10:9

Charles Swindoll once said, "It is never too late to start doing what is right."

Integrity is a quality that is often overlooked and easily put aside in a society consumed with the acquisition of things. But integrity is a reflection of our very character and, like it or not, it is best judged in private.

We must always keep our word and guard our integrity. Our children will notice.

HEAVENLY FATHER, AS YOUR CHILD I PRAY...

Dear Father, thank You for the wonderful examples of integrity I have had in my life in...

....

....

....

....

....

I ask for Your present and future guidance in developing more integrity in...

....

....

....

....

HEAVENLY FATHER, FOR MY CHILD I PRAY...

As a father, help me set the right example for my children as I...

_____

_____

_____

_____

_____

_____

Today God, help my child to develop integrity even in the smallest ways of...

_____

_____

_____

_____

_____

_____

_____

And in the future, Lord...

_____

_____

_____

_____

_____

_____

A Christian should act from within with a total disregard for the opinions of others. If a course is right, he should take it because it is right, not because he is afraid not to take it.
A. W. TOZER

A WORLD OF PEACE

And the land had peace.

JUDGES 3:30

The thought of praying for world peace is overwhelming. We all want our children and our grandchildren to live in a world without war, but human conflict is as old as man himself. Should we give up our hope and prayers for peace? Never.

Teach your child a sense of responsibility in praying for our country's leadership on all levels. Model a great belief in the power of prayer by bringing world events into family prayer time. Thank God for peace in our nation...seek it always for the world.

HEAVENLY FATHER, AS *YOUR* CHILD I PRAY...

Dear Father, thank You for peace in...

_____

_____

_____

_____

_____

_____

_____

I ask for Your present and future guidance in praying for these specific people in leadership...

_____

_____

_____

_____

_____

_____

HEAVENLY FATHER, FOR MY CHILD I PRAY...

As a father, I pray for protection not only for my own child, but children who need protection in these areas of world conflict...

Today God, may my child begin to understand Your vastness through...

And in the future, Lord...

Sometime they'll give a war and nobody will come.
CARL SANDBURG

Will the Perfect Dad Please Stand Up!

*Not that I have already obtained all this, or have already
been made perfect, but I press on.*

PHILIPPIANS 3:12

We should always strive for excellence. But perfectionism is a good idea taken to the extreme,
and as with any other extreme, somebody's going to get hurt. We must remember
not to let our quest for the best get in the way of our relationship with our children.
Sometimes the best thing is to put down the work and pick up the child.

Heavenly Father, As *Your* Child I Pray...

Dear Father, thank You for giving me the desire for excellence in...

_____

_____

_____

_____

_____

_____

I ask for Your present and future guidance in keeping my priorities straight as I...

_____

_____

_____

_____

_____

Heavenly Father, For My Child I Pray...

As a father, I pray for the ability to accept my imperfections without giving up my desire to be what You want in these areas...

Today God, help my child seek excellence without becoming a perfectionist in...

And in the future, Lord...

O God, give us serenity to accept what cannot be changed, courage to change what should be changed, and wisdom to know the difference.
REINHOLD NIEBUHR

Nowhere Else

I have been driven many times to my knees by the overwhelming conviction that I had nowhere else to go. My own wisdom, and that of all about me, seemed insufficient for the day.

ABRAHAM LINCOLN

THE BEGINNING OF WISDOM

The fear of the Lord is the beginning of wisdom;
all who follow his precepts have good understanding.
PSALM 111:10

We can acquire all the knowledge available in the world on parenting, but knowledge, without wisdom, will not provide us with all we need to be good parents. It often takes going through the "fires" of parenting to forge our knowledge into wisdom.

Tennyson said "Knowledge comes but wisdom lingers." As fathers, let us pray for the Spirit to transform all we are learning during this time in our lives into true wisdom from Him. God will grant wisdom only if we will receive it.

HEAVENLY FATHER, AS *YOUR* CHILD I PRAY...

Dear Father, thank You for being the source of all wisdom and granting us the wisdom to...

I ask for Your present and future guidance to grow in wisdom in these specific areas of my life...

HEAVENLY FATHER, FOR MY CHILD I PRAY...

As a father, I pray for parenting wisdom particularly in dealing with my child in...

Today God, help my child begin to develop wisdom, especially in these areas...

And in the future, Lord...

The road to wisdom? Well it's plain
And simple to express:
Err and err again
But less and less and less.
PAT HEIN

ACCEPT ONE ANOTHER

Accept one another, then, just as Christ accepted you,
in order to bring praise to God.

ROMANS 15:7

The issue of tolerance is often threatening, because carried to one extreme,
it can lead to indulgent leniency or even indifference to morality.
And at the other extreme, bigotry and prejudice.

But Jesus taught and lived tolerance, teaching that we should value and accept others
not based on what they do, but who they are. Regardless of our differences,
we must learn to look at each other through the eyes of the Creator of us all.

HEAVENLY FATHER, AS *YOUR* CHILD I PRAY...

Dear Father, thank You for Your loving tolerance of me, in spite of...

_____

_____

_____

_____

_____

I ask for Your present and future guidance in seeing others through Your eyes, especially
others who are different in these ways...

_____

_____

_____

_____

_____

_____

HEAVENLY FATHER, FOR MY CHILD I PRAY...

As a father, help me to model tolerance in these specific areas...

Today God, help my child begin to be more accepting of others in these areas...

And in the future, Lord...

Jesus was encouraging tolerance. Be tolerant of those who live different lifestyles.
Be tolerant of those who don't look like you, who don't dress like you, who don't care
about the things you care about, who don't vote like you. Furthermore, be tolerant of
those whose fine points of theology differ from yours, whose worship style is different.
Be tolerant of the young if you are older...and be tolerant of the aging if you are young.
CHUCK SWINDOLL

A FATHER'S PRAYER FOR PROTECTION

The Lord will keep you from all harm—he will watch over your life; the Lord will watch over your coming and going both now and forevermore.

PSALM 121:7

What a huge request. Protection from harm in an increasingly violent world. It's overwhelming to even think about as we watch the news.

The bad news is, we live in a fallen world, and it's probably not going to get much better. The good news is this...God is with us. "You can be sure that I will be with you always. I will continue with you until the end of the world" (Matthew 28:20 NIV).

Never underestimate the power of the presence of the living God. He will be there. He already is.

HEAVENLY FATHER, AS *YOUR* CHILD I PRAY...

Dear Father, thank You for these times when I saw Your hand of protection in my life...

_____

_____

_____

_____

_____

I ask for Your present and future guidance in keeping my family protected from harm...

_____

_____

_____

_____

_____

Heavenly Father, For My Child I Pray...

As a father, I pray for discernment to know when I need to be protective without being over-protective. I worry about these situations...

Today God, may my child be protected from harm as he/she goes...

And in the future, Lord...

The Lord will keep you from all harm
he will watch over your life;
the Lord will watch over your coming and going
both now and forevermore.
PSALM 121:7

NOT ALL CHILDREN ARE ATHLETES

✳

*Then the Lord said to Moses, "See, I have chosen Bezalel
and filled him with skill, ability and knowledge in all crafts."*
EXODUS 31:1–3

*How many teachers yearn to be politicians or dancers? Or how
many businessmen, want to be chefs...or science teachers...or writers?
Our creative yearnings, our talents, are gifts from God.
What we do with those talents are our gifts back to Him.*

*See your child for who he is, and encourage him to develop his God-given talents,
not just the ones you want him to have. Our talents can lead us in the direction of
our life's work, so what a waste it is when fathers encourage children in the wrong
direction because of their own fears or unfulfilled dreams.*

HEAVENLY FATHER, AS *YOUR* CHILD I PRAY...

Dear Father, thank You for the talents You've given me in these areas...

_____

_____

_____

_____

_____

_____

I ask for Your present and future guidance developing these gifts to their full potential, especially...

_____

_____

_____

_____

_____

HEAVENLY FATHER, FOR MY CHILD I PRAY...

As a father, I pray for discernment in identifying my child's God-given talents. I already see abilities in...

Today help my child develop the talents You've given...

And in the future, Lord...

The man who is born with a talent which he is meant to use,
finds his greatest happiness in using it.

TO LOVE AND BE LOVED

✳

Love one another deeply from the heart.

1 PETER 1:22

To love and to be loved are basic essentials that all of us need and desire. We spend a great deal of our existence chasing it or fighting to keep it. We glorify the feelings that it gives us and all too often forget what it takes to get there. We must never forget that the word love is not just a noun; it is also a verb which requires action. We make a decision to love, just as God made a decision to love us. We must also make the decision to accept love—from God and others.

✳

HEAVENLY FATHER, AS *YOUR* CHILD I PRAY...

Dear Father, thank You for demonstrating Your love to me in...

_____

_____

_____

_____

_____

_____

I pray that I will be a Godly example of love to my family as I...

_____

_____

_____

_____

_____

HEAVENLY FATHER, FOR MY CHILD I PRAY...

As a father, I pray for forgiveness in these areas where I have not shown love...

Today God, may my child learn to give and receive love as he/she...

And in the future, Lord...

Human things must be known to be loved:
but divine things must be loved to be known.
BLAISE PASCAL

TEACHING THEM TO GIVE

Store up for yourselves treasures in heaven.

MATTHEW 6:20

For as much joy as the act of giving brings, we have trouble believing God when He says that:
- *it is more blessed to give than to receive (Acts 20:35).*
- *whoever sows generously will reap generously (2 Corinthians 9:6).*
- *money tests the sincerity of our love to God (2 Corinthians 8:8).*

We have been told to give until it hurts. A wise man once told me that he gave until it felt good.

HEAVENLY FATHER, AS *YOUR* CHILD I PRAY...

Dear Father, thank You for giving me everything. Specifically I thank You for...

_____

_____

_____

_____

_____

_____

_____

I ask You to reveal areas where I need to give more freely, such as...

_____

_____

_____

_____

_____

_____

HEAVENLY FATHER, FOR MY CHILD I PRAY...

As a father, make me an example of a generous giver with things, words, love, praise, and...

Today God, touch my child's heart and show him/her the joy of giving in...

And in the future, Lord...

Let us give according to our incomes, lest God make our incomes match our gifts.

PETER MARSHALL

THE LADDER OF SUCCESS

O Lord, grant us success.

PSALM 118:25

Do you picture your child as "successful" in the years to come?
Does the picture include a good career, money, and a happy family?

What is God's picture of success?

God, too, wants all of His children to succeed. He just wants us to succeed in His plans,
not the plans of the world. We must trust Him to fill our child's heart with passionate plans
and daring dreams—and then watch Him begin to fulfill them! "May he give you the desire
of your heart and make all your plans succeed" (Psalm 20:4).

HEAVENLY FATHER, AS *YOUR* CHILD I PRAY...

Dear Father, thank You for the success I've had in...

I ask for Your present and future guidance in fulfilling this desire You've put in my heart...

HEAVENLY FATHER, FOR My CHILD I PRAY...

As a father, I pray for the correct definition of success specifically in...

_____

_____

_____

_____

_____

_____

Today God, help my child succeed in...

_____

_____

_____

_____

_____

_____

_____

And in the future, Lord...

_____

_____

_____

_____

_____

_____

_____

The true measure of our success will be the measure of our ability to help others.

F. B. MEYER

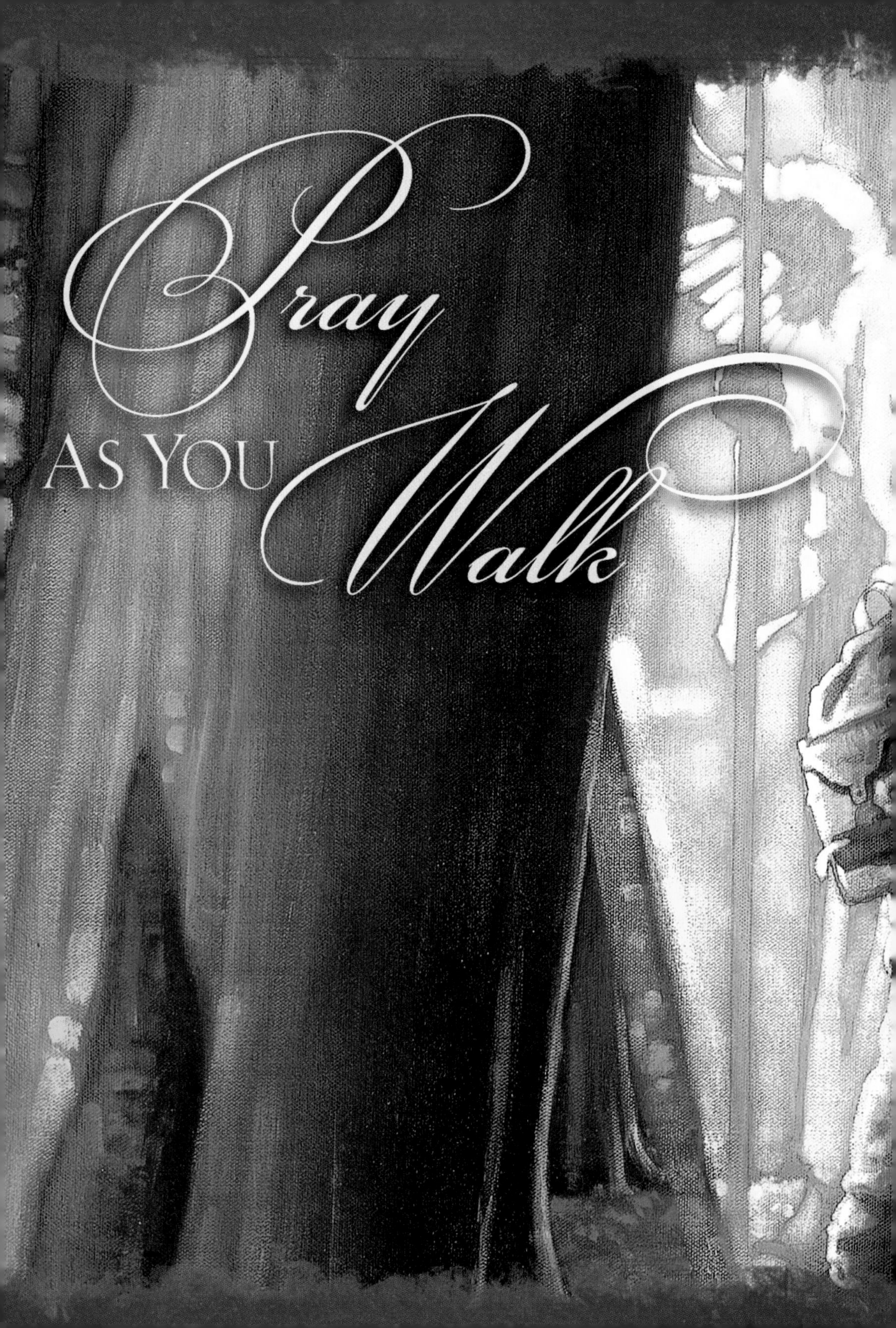
Pray
As You
Walk

Never wait for a better time or place to

talk to God. To wait until we go to church

or to our own room is to make God wait.

Pray now. God will listen as you walk.

GEORGE MACDONALD

MY CHILD'S FUTURE MATE

✳

The Lord God said, "It is not good for man to be alone.
I will make a helper suitable for him."

GENESIS 2:18

The chances are one day your child will fall in love, get married, and start a family of his or her own. The thought of this moment may make you misty-eyed or send chills down your spine!

Regardless of your feelings about it, it will probably happen. And the new son-
or daughter-in-law will become a part of your life from then on. What could be more
important than praying for this future family member every day until then?
Wouldn't you love to know that someone out there is praying for your child, too?
And if your child is already married, pray even more diligently for his or her mate.

✳

HEAVENLY FATHER, AS YOUR CHILD I PRAY...

Dear Father, thank You for my wife and these blessings she has brought into my life...

I ask for Your help in these areas as we become an example of marriage to our children...

HEAVENLY FATHER, FOR MY CHILD I PRAY...

As a father, I pray specifically to be a Godly example of a husband in the eyes of my child in these areas...

Today God, I pray for my child's spouse to be a person of...

And in the future, Lord...

Successful marriage is always a triangle: a man, a woman and God.
CECIL MYERS

MY CHILD'S SPIRITUAL GIFTS

We have different gifts, according to the grace given us.

ROMANS 12:6

*God created each of us totally unique and equipped our spirits with different characteristics
in order to accomplish His will in the world.*

*Does your child love helping others? He may have the gift of service. Or does
she love making someone's day by encouraging them? Probably the gift of encouragement.
Or does he feel the pain of others so much that it affects his mood? Mercy.*

*If you haven't already done so, learn about the spiritual gifts; it will greatly increase
your insight into your child—and yourself! (See 1 Corinthians 12.)*

HEAVENLY FATHER, AS *YOUR* CHILD I PRAY...

Dear Father, thank You for giving me the gifts of...

I ask for Your present and future guidance in using my gifts to...

HEAVENLY FATHER, FOR *My* CHILD I PRAY...

As a father, I pray for discernment in recognizing Your gifts in my child. I already see...

_____

_____

_____

_____

_____

Today God, give my child the opportunity to exercise his/her gifts as he/she...

_____

_____

_____

_____

_____

_____

And in the future, Lord...

_____

_____

_____

_____

_____

_____

Our intellect and other gifts have been given to us to be used for God's greater glory,
but sometimes they become the very god to us.
MOTHER TERESA

SHAME OR GUILT?

Let us draw near to God with a sincere heart in full assurance of faith, having our hearts sprinkled to cleanse us from a guilty conscience and having our bodies washed with pure water.

HEBREWS 10:21

Our children are, at one time or another, going to be guilty of doing something wrong. It's important as fathers to understand the difference between feeling guilty and an unhealthy sense of shame.

Our children will and should experience painful feelings of guilt—we all do in comparison to the holiness of God. But guilt should never grow into feelings of shame that are manifest as self-rejection, feelings of unworthiness, and low-self-esteem. Being ashamed in response to our undesirable actions or attitudes is a natural, God-given response, but shame shouldn't lead your child into being embarrassed of who they are.

Protect your children from the poison and lifelong implications of shame. Let them know they are accepted and loved, even when their behavior is not. This is the way God treats us.

HEAVENLY FATHER, AS *YOUR* CHILD I PRAY...

Dear Father, I confess this area in which I still battle shame...

_____

_____

_____

_____

I ask for reassurance that You have forgiven...

_____

_____

_____

_____

_____

HEAVENLY FATHER, FOR MY CHILD I PRAY...

As a father, guide me in staying away from shaming words such as...

Today, may Your Spirit convict my child when guilty, but comfort when ashamed...

And in the future, Lord...

Thank God you don't have to be flawless to be blessed! You need to have a big heart that desires and wants the will of God more than anything else in the world.

A. W. TOZER

TEACHING SELF-DISCIPLINE

✳

*The grace of God teaches us to say "No"
to ungodliness and worldly passions, and to live self-controlled,
upright and godly lives in this present age.*

TITUS 2:12

Discipline provides guidelines for a child while still giving him opportunities to make
decisions; it holds a child accountable for his actions while still conveying love and respect.
The same can be said of self-discipline, only the "parent" is ourself.
And self-discipline can be overwhelming and dangerous to us if we are not prepared to
handle the responsibility, or have not seen a good model of self-discipline.

Expecting a child to practice self-discipline when he hasn't seen discipline
is like asking a child to play in a piano recital when he hasn't even taken lessons!
We must begin with ourselves and then teach our children.

✳

HEAVENLY FATHER, AS *YOUR* CHILD I PRAY...

Dear Father, thank You for disciplining me and accepting and helping me to grow in...

_____

_____

_____

_____

_____

I ask for Your present and future guidance in leading a disciplined lifestyle, especially in...

_____

_____

_____

HEAVENLY FATHER, FOR MY CHILD I PRAY...

As a father, I pray for patience and...

Today God, help my child be self-disciplined as he/she...

And in the future, Lord...

Self-respect is the root of discipline; the sense of dignity grows
with the ability to say no to oneself.

ABRAHAM J. HESCHEL

A Child Learns Respect

Honor your father and mother—which is the first commandment with a promise.
EPHESIANS 6:2

Respect can be demanded from our children, but what we really end up with is fear of confrontation. Or respect can be nagged for, but disrespect often accompanies begging and pleading. Because respect is not easily attained; it must be earned.

Our children love us from early on, but respect develops as we use our authority as parents wisely. It requires forming a real relationship with our child—listening, making eye contact, showing him or her respect—because only when our children feel respected are they likely to respect us.

Heavenly Father, As Your Child I Pray...

Dear Father, forgive me for the times I haven't shown respect to You or Your word...

_____

_____

_____

_____

_____

_____

_____

I ask for Your present and future guidance in learning to respect and reverence You by...

_____

_____

_____

_____

Heavenly Father, For My Child I Pray...

As a father, teach me how to model for my child respect for those in authority...

Today God, help my child learn to respect...

And in the future, Lord...

*When I was fourteen, my father was so ignorant I could hardly stand to
have the old man around. But when I got to be twenty-one,
I was astonished at how much the old man had learned in seven years.*

MARK TWAIN

THE DATING GAME

Trust in the Lord with all your heart and lean not on
your own understanding; in all your ways acknowledge him,
and he will make your paths straight.

PROVERBS 3:5

Dating...help! What's a father to do? If your child is only two or twelve, you have more
time to pray and prepare, but sooner or later, you'll have to let your child go. There will
be unacceptable choices, of course. And it's a father's duty to protect his child from these.
But not every date will be a Harley–riding, chain–wearing, leather–clad freak.
Begin now preparing yourself and your child with prayer for these momentous days.

HEAVENLY FATHER, AS YOUR CHILD I PRAY...

Dear Father, thank You for loving my child even more than I do. Protect him/her in...

....

....

....

....

....

....

I ask for Your present and future guidance in preparing my child to spend time socially with others. Specifically, to be...

....

....

....

....

....

HEAVENLY FATHER, FOR MY CHILD I PRAY...

As a father, I pray not to fear my child's teenage years, but to prepare for them daily by...

_____

_____

_____

_____

_____

_____

_____

Today, help my child learn to develop the social skills of...

_____

_____

_____

_____

_____

_____

_____

And in the future, Lord...

_____

_____

_____

_____

_____

_____

_____

The best way to keep children at home is to create a pleasant atmosphere—
and to let the air out of their tires.
BARBARA JOHNSON

SUFFERING SIBLINGS

✳

*Joseph said to his brothers, "You intended to harm me,
but God intended it for good. So then, don't be afraid.
I will provide for you and your children." And he reassured
them and spoke kindly to them.*

GENESIS 50:20, 21

If you have more than one child, you already know about sibling rivalry. Sibling rivalry often occurs because our children have conflicting ideas about how they want to be treated. They want to be treated the same as the oldest, and the same as the youngest, yet different from all the rest!

Although disturbing, it's normal for siblings to whine and complain about each other. They, like us, are often just venting. Their idea is to get the parents involved, so stay out of it as often as you can.

Teach them that you love them all the same, but treat them differently depending upon what you believe is appropriate for each child. Much as you may want to, not every child can be treated alike.

✳

HEAVENLY FATHER, AS YOUR CHILD I PRAY...

Dear Father, thank You for every member of our family...

....

....

....

....

....

I ask for Your present and future guidance in showing love to each child and keeping our family close especially during...

....

....

....

....

HEAVENLY FATHER, FOR MY CHILD I PRAY...

As a father, I pray for discernment to know when and when not to intervene in...

Today God, help my children begin to appreciate these things about each other...

And in the future, Lord, I pray for loving relationships between...

A family is the place where principles are hammered and honed
on the anvil of everyday living.
CHUCK SWINDOLL

I'LL DO IT TOMORROW

The foolish wedding guests procrastinated and did not buy their oil soon enough. When they left to buy more, the door was shut.
MATTHEW 25:1–13

Procrastination has been described as "slow suicide," and for good reason. It neutralizes our motivation, zaps our energy, and leaves us with an overwhelming sense of guilt.

We are the "extra push" our children need when they procrastinate. And although they sometimes whine and complain, our consistent "push"—to pick up after themselves, finish their work, or feed the dog—keeps their world in order.
As we learn to conquer procrastination, so will they.

HEAVENLY FATHER, AS YOUR CHILD I PRAY...

Dear Father, I pray for the "extra push" I need to face these unpleasant tasks this week...

I ask for Your future guidance in facing procrastination in these specific areas of my life...

HEAVENLY FATHER, FOR MY CHILD I PRAY...

As a father, give me wisdom in helping my child deal with these areas of procrastination that are already evident in his/her life...

Today, may Your Spirit be where I cannot and guide him/her in these tasks...

And in the future, Lord...

Yesterday is a canceled check, and tomorrow is a promissory note.
But today is cash, ready for us to spend in living.
BARBARA JOHNSON

Because of His generosity, God grants many things to us and our children. But for the sake of our good, He desires to bestow certain things on us only when we ask. He does this so that we will develop more confidence in approaching Him, and will recognize Him as the author of every good thing.

THOMAS AQUINAS

Every Good Thing

PRIDE GOES FIRST

Pride goes before destruction, a haughty spirit before a fall.
PROVERBS 16:18

"I can do it by myself" is a familiar phrase to all fathers. Often, as adults, we demonstrate the same prideful attitude toward our Heavenly Father. This is the "negative pride" that C. S. Lewis called the utmost evil, a complete "anti-God" state of mind.

One of the challenges facing us as fathers lies in modeling to our children a strong sense of self-assurance and competence, without crossing the line into arrogance and pridefulness. Pride refuses to allow a humble dependence upon our Heavenly Father. It also doesn't allow us to recognize and demonstrate our appreciation for God's part in bestowing His gifts and talents upon us.

Recognize your strength, your talents, your gifts. Encourage your children to do the same, and always thankfully and humbly acknowledge the Source.

HEAVENLY FATHER, AS YOUR CHILD I PRAY...

Dear Father, forgive my pridefulness in the area of...

I ask for Your present and future guidance in becoming more humble and...

Heavenly Father, For My Child I Pray...

As a father, guide me in modeling humility as I...

Today, help my child learn the difference between humility versus weakness in...

And in the future, Lord...

As long as you are proud you cannot know God. A proud man is always looking down on things and people; and, of course, as long as you are looking down, you cannot see something that is above you.

C. S. LEWIS

THE GIFT OF PEACE

Peace I leave with you; my peace I give you.
JOHN 14:27

*Peace could be defined as absence of turmoil. Sounds good, but genuine peace is more than that.
Peace cannot be bought...it cannot be taught...it cannot be imposed on us.
True authentic peace is a gift from God.*

*It may come at a quiet moment through the gesture of a friend, or it may come during a time
of deep grief. During our prayers or on our morning run. In the midst of laughter or tears,
joys and sorrows...peace comes to those who want it and will allow God to give it.*

HEAVENLY FATHER, AS *YOUR* CHILD I PRAY...

Dear Father, thank You for Your Ultimate Gift of Peace for my life...

I ask for daily peace for my family, even in the midst of...

Heavenly Father, For My Child I Pray...

As a father, I pray for peace in the knowledge that I'm doing my best even though...

Today God, help my child have a peaceful spirit as he/she goes...

And in the future, Lord...

Sowing seeds of peace is like sowing beans. You don't know why it works;
you just know it does.
MAX LUCADO

Muddling Through Mistakes

As for God, his way is perfect.
PSALM 18:30

We live in an imperfect world filled with imperfect people.
Mistakes will be made—Grandmother's china broken, balls fumbled, words misspelled.
But developing a healthy acceptance of our own imperfection and the imperfection of those
around us is imperative in dealing with life.

We must accept our own mistakes, learn from them, and occasionally laugh at ourselves.
Accept your children's mistakes...and let them know it's okay.
After all, God is still the only member of the family who doesn't "mess up."

✳

Heavenly Father, As Your Child I Pray...

Dear Father, thank You for Your consistent patience in these areas of my life where I have
continually made mistakes...

I ask for Your present and future guidance in trying to learn from my mistakes of...

HEAVENLY FATHER, FOR MY CHILD I PRAY...

As a father, I pray for patience when dealing with my mistakes and my child's mistakes in...

Today, help my child to learn the difference between imperfection and "sloppy work" as he/she...

And in the future, Lord...

There is nothing wrong with making mistakes. Just don't respond with encores.
ANONYMOUS

MAKING A CHILD'S MEMORIES

I always thank my God as I remember you.

PHILEMON 4

We are so often overwhelmed in parenting that we forget to pause a minute and thank God for the beautiful gift of our children. Stop every now and then and remember the first time you saw that precious little face, or the first time that little finger curled around yours, or the first giggle.

And remember, you are in control of your memories. Today's activities are the stuff of tomorrow's memories. Take time out today to make some happy ones. This week, go ahead and plan that special activity—and take plenty of pictures!

HEAVENLY FATHER, AS YOUR CHILD I PRAY...

Dear Father, thank You for my family and the memory of...

I ask for Your present and future guidance in making many happy memories in...

HEAVENLY FATHER, FOR MY CHILD I PRAY...

As a father, when I'm having a horrible day, please remind me of...

Today God, help my child make a happy memory as we...

And in the future, Lord...

I love these little people; and it is not a slight thing when they,
who are so fresh from God, love us.
CHARLES DICKENS

A FATHER'S GIFT OF INDEPENDENCE

✳

Be imitators of God, therefore,
as dearly loved children and live a life of love.

EPHESIANS 5:1

For fathers, letting go is a lifelong process. From your baby's first night in his own room,
to riding his bike down the street, and then taking the car out on Friday night...
the letting go never ends. And it shouldn't. Because as tough as it is to do,
not letting go leads to unhealthy dependence.

Although letting go is perhaps one of the most difficult aspects of parenting, rest assured that
our Heavenly Father understands. With the power of the universe at His right hand,
He waits and watches as we blunder around, often following our own path instead of His.
Try to keep this in mind each time you unclench your fist, open your hand, and let your child go.

✳

HEAVENLY FATHER, AS YOUR CHILD I PRAY...

Dear Father, thank You for giving me this child that I love in so many ways...

I ask for Your future guidance and preparation for this difficult task, already knowing I may
have a hard time with...

HEAVENLY FATHER, FOR MY CHILD I PRAY...

As a father, give me wisdom to guide my child into growing healthy wings, and work on these areas in my heart...

Today, may Your Spirit begin to work to develop healthy dependence and independence in these areas of my child's life...

And in the future, Lord...

There are only two lasting bequests we can hope to give our children.
One of these is roots, the other, wings.
HODDING CARTER

PROTECTION FROM HARMFUL INFLUENCES

✳

Holy Father, protect them by the power of your name. My prayer is not that you take them out of the world but that you protect them.

JOHN 17:11, 15

As fathers, we are already aware of the multitude of powerful, negative, and harmful influences in the world. They're either in the school, the neighborhood, or the mall. Some are minor, some are scary.

But as faithful fathers, this is the test of our faith. Because as absolutely terrifying as it is to send our children out into the world each day, we must do it with confidence, we must believe the powerful promises of the God we serve, who says, "Fear not, for I am with you."

HEAVENLY FATHER, AS *YOUR* CHILD I PRAY...

Dear Father, thank You for protecting me all these years from...

_____

_____

_____

_____

_____

I ask for Your present and future guidance in keeping my family safe from these influences...

_____

_____

_____

_____

HEAVENLY FATHER, FOR MY CHILD I PRAY...

As a father, I pray for the wisdom to recognize the potential harmful influences of...

Today God, may my child be protected from harmful influences as he/she goes...

And in the future, Lord...

The greater the evil, the greater the opportunity to fashion out of it everlasting good.
HANNAH HURNARD

LIVING IN THE WILL

✳

The man who does the will of God lives forever.

1 JOHN 2:15

The world calls the fulfillment of our life's purpose destiny. As Christians,
we call it staying within God's will for our life. And we readily admit wanting
God's will for our children. But what if God's plan isn't what we plan,
or isn't comfortable for us, or even takes our children far away?

As fathers, gently guiding our children toward God's path requires wisdom and a
willingness to let them follow their own "bent" in life. And ultimately the best way
to pray may be that—in spite of our parental fears, worries, and blind spots—
the will of God will be accomplished anyway!

✳

HEAVENLY FATHER, AS *YOUR* CHILD I PRAY...

Dear Father, thank You for revealing to me Your will for my life in these areas...

_____

_____

_____

_____

_____

_____

I ask for Your present and future guidance in keeping myself and my family in the center of
Your will as we...

_____

_____

_____

_____

_____

Heavenly Father, For My Child I Pray...

As a father, I pray for wisdom modeling to my child what it means to follow Your will in these ways...

Today God, may my child's heart be tender and open to direction from Your Spirit in...

And in the future, Lord...

Like anybody I would like to live a long life. Longevity has its place.
But I'm not concerned about that now. I just want to do God's will.
MARTIN LUTHER KING, JR.

God's way of answering the

PRAYER

Christian's prayer for more

HOPE

patience, experience, hope,

and love often is to test him

TEST

with the chisel of affliction.

RICHARD CECIL

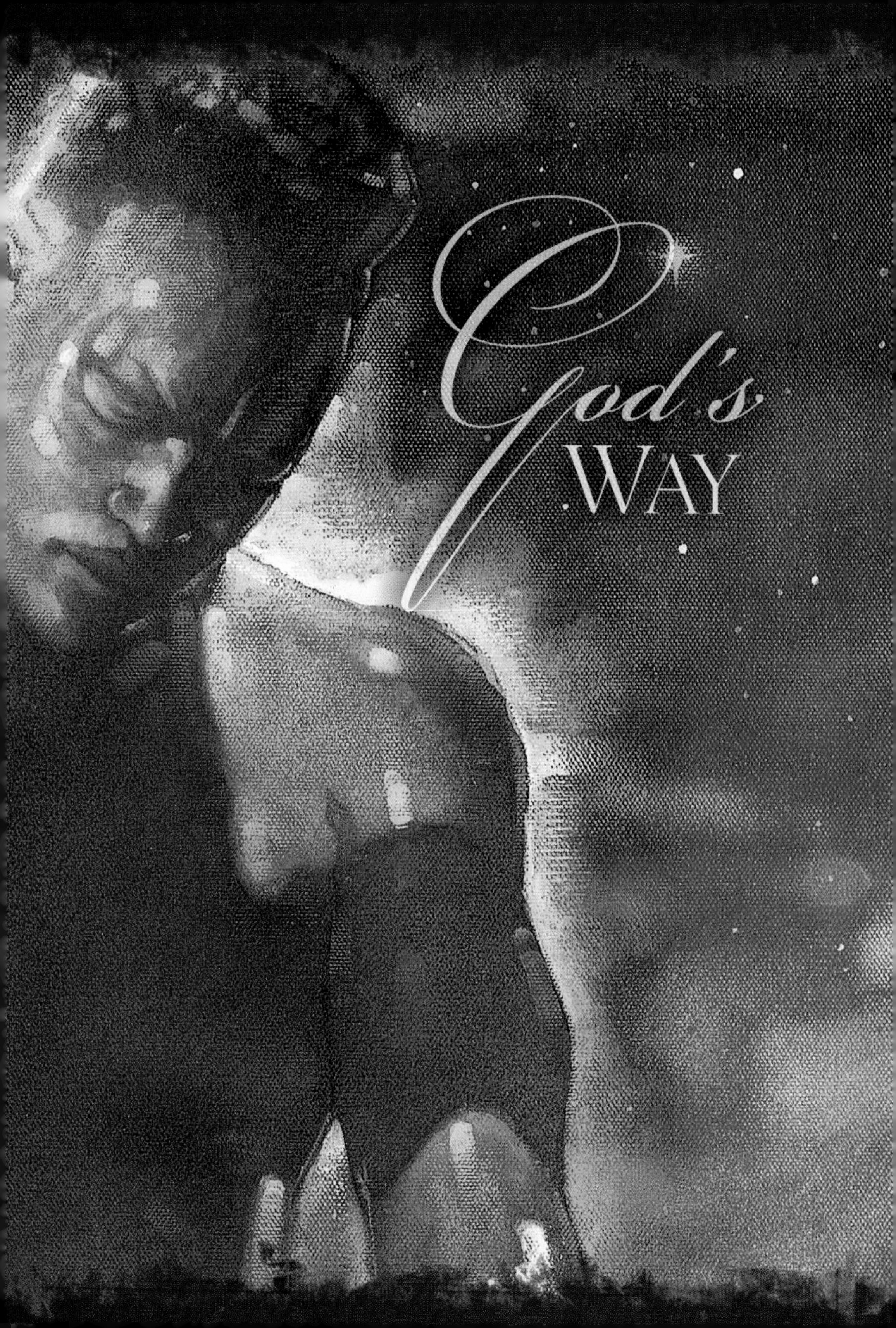
God's
WAY

MY CHILD'S FRIENDS

Dear friends, now we are children of God.
Do not let anyone lead you astray.

1 JOHN 3:2, 7

Our friendships can bring us great joy or great troubles, depending upon whom we've chosen as friends. Do you ever consider moving far away and starting over?
Good or bad, one thing is for sure...friendships are never easy. For adults or children.

Whom our children choose for friends is a tremendous area of concern. We all know the power of peer pressure and the influence others can have on their lives. And, as much as we want to hold "best-friend try-outs" for our children, we simply can't. We can, however, provide opportunities for them to meet great friends, but who they choose is ultimately up to them.

And the most important thing we can do is to pray.

HEAVENLY FATHER, AS YOUR CHILD I PRAY...

Dear Father, thank You for these people who have become good friends in my life...

_____

_____

_____

_____

_____

I ask for Your present and future guidance with these specific friendships in my life...

_____

_____

_____

_____

_____

HEAVENLY FATHER, FOR MY CHILD I PRAY...

As a father, I need help in dealing with this aspect of my child's friendships...

_____

_____

_____

_____

_____

_____

Today God, help my child to seek friends who are...

_____

_____

_____

_____

_____

_____

_____

And in the future, Lord...

_____

_____

_____

_____

_____

_____

The fingers of God touch your life when you touch a friend.
MARY DAWN HUGHES

TEACHING THEM TO FORGIVE

✳

Bear with each other and forgive whatever grievances you may have against one another. Forgive as the Lord forgave you.

COLOSSIANS 3:13

We all believe in forgiveness, but we often attach our own conditions to forgiving—
"I'll forgive him if or when...." Christ, however, didn't tell us it would be nice or thoughtful
to forgive. Instead, He commanded us to forgive as we have been forgiven. Period.

Truthfully, there are people we don't want to "let off the hook." Because if we release them
from what they've done to us or someone else, who will carry out the judgment they deserve?
We should consider letting God judge. Not only because He's commanded us to, but because
not forgiving makes us spiritually ill and separates us from our loving Father.

✳

HEAVENLY FATHER, AS *YOUR* CHILD I PRAY...

Dear Father, thank You for forgiving me of...

I ask for Your present and future guidance in helping me to resove these areas of
unforgiveness in my heart...

HEAVENLY FATHER, FOR MY CHILD I PRAY...

As a father, make me more Christlike in granting, receiving and modeling forgiveness in the areas of...

Today God, help my child learn to develop forgiveness by...

And in the future, Lord...

We all agree that forgiveness is a beautiful idea until we have to practice it.
C. S. LEWIS

CONTENTED CHILDREN

✳

But godliness with contentment is great gain.
1 TIMOTHY 6:6

Praying for contentment for our children is easy to neglect, because the idea of contentment scares us. Is it possible we're afraid that if our children become content, they'll be underachievers who never quite reach their potential, maybe even moving back home one day!

True contentment isn't contradictory to growth and drive, but rather a necessary part of it. Without contentment, we end up on an endless search for "ourselves," never able to appreciate and live in the here and now.

Paul said, "I have learned the secret of being content in any and every situation, whether well fed or hungry, whether living in plenty or in want" (Philippians 4:12).

The key words here are..."I have learned."

✳

HEAVENLY FATHER, AS YOUR CHILD I PRAY...

Dear Father, thank You for bringing me to the place of contentment in these areas...

_____

_____

_____

_____

_____

I ask for Your present and future guidance in developing an attitude of contentment about...

_____

_____

_____

_____

HEAVENLY FATHER, FOR MY CHILD I PRAY...

As a father, I want to model contentment specifically for my child in this area...

Today God, may my child learn to be content in...

And in the future, Lord...

God made me to be real, to be honest, to be open. To never compare myself to you,
but to strive to become my own best person. To have character and dignity.
ANN KIEMAL ANDERSON

HABITS DON'T JUST HAPPEN

✳

Submit yourselves, then, to God. Resist the devil, and he will flee from you. Come near to God and he will come near to you.

JAMES 4:7, 8

Habits...even mentioning the word brings a negative image to our minds. Perhaps because most of us find ourselves spending more time wrestling with bad habits than we do in developing good ones.

The best we can pray for our children is protection from the opportunities to develop bad habits—especially those of addiction. Pray for God's Spirit to empower your children to stop destructive behaviors before they become prisoners of them.

✳

HEAVENLY FATHER, AS *YOUR* CHILD I PRAY...

Dear Father, thank You for these models of good habits in my life...

_____

_____

_____

_____

_____

_____

_____

I ask for Your help in breaking these bad habits I still wrestle with...

_____

_____

_____

_____

Heavenly Father, For My Child I Pray...

As a father, I ask for wisdom in helping my child establish the good habits of...

Today God, may my child be protected from these things which could become habitual in his his/her life...

And in the future, Lord...

The chains of habit are generally too small to be felt until
they are too strong to be broken.
SAMUEL JOHNSON

ANXIOUS PRAYERS

✳

*Do not be anxious about anything, but in everything,
by prayer and petition with thanksgiving, present your requests to God.*
PHILIPPIANS 4:6

What made you anxious when you were young? Like many of us, it may have been whom you were going to hang out with at lunch, or whether or not you could borrow the car for a big date. You probably didn't worry about being shot and killed at school. Or you weren't often distressed because one of your friends overdosed on heroin or committed suicide. Today's children are.

Constant anxiety can be a root cause in illness and psychological disorders. If our children are going to remain healthy and whole, their feelings of anxiety need to be expressed, talked about, and dealt with. Anxiety and prayer are two great opposing forces in the Christian life. Prayer, petition, and thanksgiving are God's answer to anxiety. We must teach and model this valuable truth to our children continually.

✳

HEAVENLY FATHER, AS *YOUR* CHILD I PRAY...

Dear Father, thank You for being the God of all comfort who...

_____

_____

_____

_____

_____

Help me to turn my anxieties over to You about...

_____

_____

_____

_____

HEAVENLY FATHER, FOR MY CHILD I PRAY...

As a father, help me be more observant of my child's anxieties about...

Today God, help my child share any anxieties of...

And in the future, Lord...

Anxiety is the natural result when our hopes are centered in anything
short of God and His will for us.
BILLY GRAHAM

TROUBLESOME TIMES

*Hear my prayer, O Lord. In the day of my trouble
I will call to you, for you will answer me.*

PSALM 86:6, 7

Job said it best, "I escaped by the skin of my teeth" (Job 19:20).

In this life, we will encounter trouble and adversity. And it's through these hard times we are given a chance to learn and grow. Whether we become bitter or better through them is up to us.

As our children face the deep waters of adversity, we will struggle with the question of whether to jump in and bail them out, or let them learn to swim. Only God knows a father's place in each situation. Only in asking will we have the wisdom to know as well.

HEAVENLY FATHER, AS YOUR CHILD I PRAY...

Dear Father, thank You for teaching me these lessons through the hard times...

_____

_____

_____

_____

_____

I ask for Your present and future guidance in surviving the difficult areas of...

_____

_____

_____

_____

_____

Heavenly Father, For My Child I Pray...

As a father, I pray for discernment in knowing how and when to help my child face the adversity of...

Today God, may my child be prepared in some small way for facing these difficult life times...

And in the future, Lord...

Funny thing how trouble acts differently in people; it's like hot weather—
it sours milk but sweetens apples.
JOSEPH C. LINCOLN

THE LION LURKS

Be self-controlled and alert. Your enemy the devil prowls around like a roaring lion looking for someone to devour.

1 PETER 5:8

If we believe in God's Word, then we must also believe in the powerful evil forces at work in the world. While our enemy the devil prowls around like a roaring lion looking for someone to devour, fathers have the spiritual authority to command the evil one to leave our children alone.

Evil is a very real and present danger. Satan has the power to destroy us if we let him.
Claim the authority of Christ over yourself and your children.
Stand steady and strong against this evil one.

HEAVENLY FATHER, AS YOUR CHILD I PRAY...

Dear Father, thank You for Your victory on the cross and the power of Your name in standing against evil...

_____

_____

_____

_____

_____

_____

_____

I ask for an alert spirit when the evil one is prowling around my family and friends. Help me to...

_____

_____

_____

_____

HEAVENLY FATHER, FOR MY CHILD I PRAY...

As a father, I pray for spiritual discernment, especially in...

Today God, may my child be protected from the evil one in these areas...

And in the future, Lord...

Our adversary is a master strategist, forever fogging up
our minds with smoke screens.
CHUCK SWINDOLL

JUST BE PATIENT!

Be patient with everyone.

1 THESSALONIANS 5:14

For the first four-and-a-half years of its life, the Chinese bamboo tree lives underground, establishing a root system. This root system then allows the tree to grow ninety feet in its fifth year!

Patience is not idleness. It's growing at the pace God has determined for each of us. We must not try to rush ahead and speed up the process to meet our own agenda. As fathers, let us rest in the truth that, like the Chinese bamboo tree, God's timing is also perfect for us.

HEAVENLY FATHER, AS *YOUR* CHILD I PRAY...

Dear Father, thank You for being so patient with me in these areas...

I ask for Your present and future guidance as I learn to be more patient in...

HEAVENLY FATHER, FOR MY CHILD I PRAY...

As a father, help me model patience as I...

Today God, help my child begin to develop more patience as he/she...

And in the future, Lord...

Teach us, O Lord, the discipline of patience, for to wait is often harder than to work.
PETER MARSHALL

AUTHENTIC Men

AFFECTION
HUG
HELP

Authentic men aren't afraid to show affection, release their feelings, hug their children, cry when they're sad, admit it when they're wrong, and ask for help when they need it.

CHUCK SWINDOLL

THE WORK OF PERSEVERANCE

*Perseverance must finish its work so that you may be
more mature and complete, not lacking anything.*

JAMES 1:4

*Perseverance. Easy to say, hard to do. Stick with it...don't give up...never say die.
I guess they've never been in your shoes, huh?*

*Persevering is tough, but many times we don't have a choice. It's like climbing up a difficult
mountain trail and then wondering how in the world we're ever going to make it back down.
We just have to.*

*Parenting is the same way. Our children are here with us for many more years.
There is no going back...but there is perseverance through it. And what was it the Apostle
Paul said would come from perseverance? Oh, yes...character.*

HEAVENLY FATHER, AS *YOUR* CHILD I PRAY...

Dear Father, thank You for strength You've given me to persevere in these areas...

I ask for forgiveness because I have given up too quickly in...

HEAVENLY FATHER, FOR MY CHILD I PRAY...

As a father, make me a Godly example of perseverance in this area...

Today God, help my child begin to develop perseverance in these areas...

And in the future, Lord...

*When we do the best we can, we never know what miracle is
wrought in our life, or in the life of another.*
HELEN KELLER

PEOPLE OF PURITY

But among you there must not be even a hint of sexual immorality, or of any kind of impurity, or of greed, because these are improper for God's holy people.

EPHESIANS 5:3

Sexual impurity is rampant in our nation; it's rampant both among adults and teens as well. Although we'd rather hide from it or deny it exists, we can't.

If we want our child to stay sexually pure, it's going to have to be a team effort. Sex must be discussed and our child supported, warned, and informed. It's not a battle we'll be able to fight from the sidelines. To win this battle, we will have to jump into the trenches. We can't afford to be too embarrassed to discuss sex. Look around. The world is not.

HEAVENLY FATHER, AS YOUR CHILD I PRAY...

Dear Father, thank You for loving my children even more than I do. I know You care about their...

_____

_____

_____

_____

_____

_____

I ask for Your present and future guidance as our family seeks to avoid the impurities of...

_____

_____

_____

_____

HEAVENLY FATHER, FOR MY CHILD I PRAY...

As a father, help me to model purity as I...

Today God, may my child be protected from the impure areas of...

And in the future, Lord...

We may indeed, be sure that perfect chastity—like perfect charity—will not be attained by any merely human efforts. You must ask for God's help.
C. S. LEWIS

DELIVERED FROM FEAR

*

*I sought the Lord, and he answered me;
he delivered me from all my fears.*

PSALM 34:4

Fear is universal. We learn how to fear at an early age, and quite often, our fears grow along with us—even to the point of paralyzing us and preventing us from letting God fulfill His purposes through us.

God doesn't want us to live with our hearts gripped by the cold hand of fear. "I have not given you a spirit of fear, but of power and love and of a sound mind" (2 Timothy 1:7 NKJV).

As fathers, let us all learn this verse and teach it to our children.
God can and will help us conquer fear. All we have to do is ask.

HEAVENLY FATHER, AS YOUR CHILD I PRAY...

Dear Father, thank You for conquering sin and death and making it possible to live without the fear of...

_____

_____

_____

_____

_____

_____

I ask for Your present and future guidance in releasing these fears to You...

_____

_____

_____

_____

HEAVENLY FATHER, FOR MY CHILD I PRAY...

As a father, my greatest fear is...

Today God, help my child to be confident and bold as he/she...

And in the future, Lord...

We master fear through faith—faith in the worthwhileness of life
and the trustworthiness of God.
JOSHUA LOTH LIEBMAN

My Work Is Not Who I Am

✳

*Whatever you do, work at it with all your heart,
as working for the Lord, not for men.*

COLOSSIANS 3:23

As men, we are often defined by what we do to make a living. As a result, we take pride
in our work and it takes a great deal of our time. While God expects us to provide for our
family and to give our employers our best, He does not define us by our jobs and does not want
us to neglect our families. He wants us to be husbands to our wives and fathers to our children.

✳

Heavenly Father, As Your Child I Pray...

Dear Father, thank You for my job because...

_____

_____

_____

_____

_____

_____

_____

Help me balance all the demands of...

_____

_____

_____

_____

_____

HEAVENLY FATHER, FOR MY CHILD I PRAY...

As a father and husband, I pray for direction in...

Today God, help my child to know how much I love him/her. Help me show it by...

And in the future, Lord...

Workaholics commit slow suicide by refusing to allow
the child inside of them to play.

DR. LAURENCE SUSSER

ADJUSTING TO CHANGE

I the Lord do not change.

MALACHI 3:6

Is it possible that we live in such a transient society that we underestimate the effect change has upon our spirits and the spirits of our children?

Anatole France said, "All changes, even the most longed for, have their melancholy, for what we leave behind us is a part of ourselves; we must die to one life before we can enter another."

Change, however small, brings with it a sense of grief, a time of readjusting and contemplating life. Understand this as your first or last child leaves for kindergarten. Understand this in your children as their friends move away. Change changes you. As fathers, we must help our children adjust and make transitions.

HEAVENLY FATHER, AS *YOUR* CHILD I PRAY...

Dear Father, thank You for being the Unchanging One who will never change...

I also thank You for sticking close to me during these times of change in my life...

HEAVENLY FATHER, FOR MY CHILD I PRAY...

As a father, I pray for compassion and empathy as my child undergoes these changes...

Today God, may my child be prepared in some way to face...

And in the future, Lord...

But as you grow and change, some things will stay the same.
I'll always love you. I'll always hug you. I'll always be on your side.
And I want you to know that...just in case you ever wonder.

MAX LUCADO

A Child's Questions

✴

Make every effort to add to your faith goodness;
and to goodness, knowledge; and to knowledge, self-control.

2 PETER 1:5, 6

From the moment we learn to speak, we ask questions. We were born with a thirst
for knowledge. One of the greatest gifts we can give our children is taking time to listen to
question, after question, after question...and leading them into finding the answers.
Don't assume your child's teachers can possibly scratch the surface of all of the knowledge
available in these present times. Teaching our children requires us all.

✴

HEAVENLY FATHER, AS *YOUR* CHILD I PRAY...

Dear Father, thank You for revealing Yourself to us and giving us knowledge of Your...

_____

_____

_____

_____

_____

_____

I ask for Your present and future guidance in continuing to grow and learn, especially in...

_____

_____

_____

_____

_____

HEAVENLY FATHER, FOR MY CHILD I PRAY...

As a father, I pray for the ability to increase my child's curiosity and thirst for knowledge by...

_____

_____

_____

_____

_____

_____

_____

Today God, may my child learn something that will inspire him/her in...

_____

_____

_____

_____

_____

_____

_____

_____

_____

And in the future, Lord...

_____

_____

_____

_____

_____

_____

_____

_____

Knowledge begins with wondering. Set a child to wondering and you
have put him on the road to understanding.
SAMUEL P. LANGLEY

To Love the Lord Our God

Love the Lord your God with all your heart
and with all your soul and all your mind.

MATTHEW 22:37

After all the parenting books are finished and you've heard all the advice from older parents,
there's still just one thing that really matters. We must help our children come to know
and love the Lord Almighty and His Son Jesus Christ.

If our children miss the music lessons or tennis or the honor roll, life will go on. If they miss
God, they have missed everything. Pray for your child to love God. Pray together with your
child to God and help him/her to know the Lord firsthand. It's the only thing that matters.

Heavenly Father, As Your Child I Pray...

Dear Father, thank You for the gift of Your Son who has blessed me with...

_____

_____

_____

_____

_____

_____

_____

I ask for Your help in loving You more, especially Your...

_____

_____

_____

_____

_____

_____

Heavenly Father, For My Child I Pray...

As a father, I pray for the ability to show my child how much I love You. Let me show it in...

_____
_____
_____
_____
_____
_____
_____
_____

Today God, may my child know how much You love him/her, and grow to love Your...

_____
_____
_____
_____
_____
_____
_____
_____

And in the future, Lord...

_____
_____
_____
_____
_____
_____
_____

There is nothing we can do to make God love us more!
There is nothing we can do to make God love us less!
His love is unconditional, impartial, everlasting, infinite, perfect!